This notebook
belongs to

Hi,
Congratulations on getting this book! You will love it!
Nice to meet you - I'm Bex Beltran.
I'm a superfan of journals, workbooks and notebooks and I hope you are too!
I'm also a podcast host, coach and teacher.
You can find out more about what I create and offer at http://bexb.org/
You can listen to the podcast, Release Your Resistance, wherever you
usually listen to podcasts.

Shop other journals, workbooks and notebooks and get more info at http://bexb.org/shopjournals

Follow me socially at
@bex_beltran
https://www.facebook.com/ReleaseYourResistance

Copyright Beltran Creative Services LLC. All rights reserved. No part of this publication may be reproduced, distributed, or transmitted in any form or by any means, including photocopying, recording, or other electronic or mechanical methods, without the prior written permission of the publisher, except in the case of brief quotations embodied in critical reviews and certain other noncommercial uses permitted by copyright law.

FEEL YOUR FEELINGS.

Feelings are so interesting and so central to the human experience.
We know our actions are influenced by how we are feeling because of what we're thinking.
We also know that the only reason we ever do anything is because of how we think we will feel.

Even though we intellectually know these things, sometimes it's easy to forget and just get swept up in our feelings as if we didn't have any input or influence.

A feeling is a vibration in the body.
Some of those vibrations feel better than others.
For example, when you feel guilt or shame, you might notice a sense of tightening. You might notice a lump in your throat.

On the other hand, when feeling delight or relief, you probably notice a loosening in your body. You might even catch yourself exhaling, or you might notice a smile, a change of facial expression.

Be curious and compassionate about your feelings.
Notice your feelings, get curious about them,
ask some questions about them, allow them.
Don't judge yourself for feeling.

Don't judge the feeling as being bad or unwanted.
Just settle in and allow feelings without resisting, while remembering:
"I'm just experiencing this and I'm just feeling these vibrations right now in my body."

Now it's your turn.
Check in with yourself. How do you feel? Describe it.
Can you be curious about it?
Can you just be with that feeling and allow it?

date:

What specific feeling are you feeling right now?

Describe it. Where is it in your body?
Is it fast, slow, heavy, light, dense, floaty, hot, cold?

What thoughts are you thinking that are creating that feeling for you?

Narrow it down to a specific sentence:

Is that sentence factual (or an opinion)?
Is it true? Is it helpful to continue thinking it?

How would you like to feel?

What thought could you think to feel that way?

Reflections:

date:

What specific feeling are you feeling right now?

Describe it. Where is it in your body?
Is it fast, slow, heavy, light, dense, floaty, hot, cold?

What thoughts are you thinking that are creating that feeling for you?

Narrow it down to a specific sentence:

Is that sentence factual (or an opinion)?
Is it true? Is it helpful to continue thinking it?

How would you like to feel?

What thought could you think to feel that way?

Reflections:

date:

What specific feeling are you feeling right now?

Describe it. Where is it in your body?
Is it fast, slow, heavy, light, dense, floaty, hot, cold?

What thoughts are you thinking that are creating that feeling for you?

Narrow it down to a specific sentence:

Is that sentence factual (or an opinion)?
Is it true? Is it helpful to continue thinking it?

How would you like to feel?

What thought could you think to feel that way?

Reflections:

date:

What specific feeling are you feeling right now?

Describe it. Where is it in your body?
Is it fast, slow, heavy, light, dense, floaty, hot, cold?

What thoughts are you thinking that are creating that feeling for you?

Narrow it down to a specific sentence:

Is that sentence factual (or an opinion)?
Is it true? Is it helpful to continue thinking it?

How would you like to feel?

What thought could you think to feel that way?

Reflections:

date:

What specific feeling are you feeling right now?

Describe it. Where is it in your body?
Is it fast, slow, heavy, light, dense, floaty, hot, cold?

What thoughts are you thinking that are creating that feeling for you?

Narrow it down to a specific sentence:

Is that sentence factual (or an opinion)?
Is it true? Is it helpful to continue thinking it?

How would you like to feel?

What thought could you think to feel that way?

Reflections:

date:

What specific feeling are you feeling right now?

Describe it. Where is it in your body?
Is it fast, slow, heavy, light, dense, floaty, hot, cold?

What thoughts are you thinking that are creating that feeling for you?

Narrow it down to a specific sentence:

Is that sentence factual (or an opinion)?
Is it true? Is it helpful to continue thinking it?

How would you like to feel?

What thought could you think to feel that way?

Reflections:

date:

What specific feeling are you feeling right now?

Describe it. Where is it in your body?
Is it fast, slow, heavy, light, dense, floaty, hot, cold?

What thoughts are you thinking that are creating that feeling for you?

Narrow it down to a specific sentence:

Is that sentence factual (or an opinion)?
Is it true? Is it helpful to continue thinking it?

How would you like to feel?

What thought could you think to feel that way?

Reflections:

date:

What specific feeling are you feeling right now?

Describe it. Where is it in your body?
Is it fast, slow, heavy, light, dense, floaty, hot, cold?

What thoughts are you thinking that are creating that feeling for you?

Narrow it down to a specific sentence:

Is that sentence factual (or an opinion)?
Is it true? Is it helpful to continue thinking it?

How would you like to feel?

What thought could you think to feel that way?

Reflections:

date:

What specific feeling are you feeling right now?

Describe it. Where is it in your body?
Is it fast, slow, heavy, light, dense, floaty, hot, cold?

What thoughts are you thinking that are creating that feeling for you?

Narrow it down to a specific sentence:

Is that sentence factual (or an opinion)?
Is it true? Is it helpful to continue thinking it?

How would you like to feel?

What thought could you think to feel that way?

Reflections:

date:

What specific feeling are you feeling right now?

Describe it. Where is it in your body?
Is it fast, slow, heavy, light, dense, floaty, hot, cold?

What thoughts are you thinking that are creating that feeling for you?

Narrow it down to a specific sentence:

Is that sentence factual (or an opinion)?
Is it true? Is it helpful to continue thinking it?

How would you like to feel?

What thought could you think to feel that way?

Reflections:

date:

What specific feeling are you feeling right now?

Describe it. Where is it in your body?
Is it fast, slow, heavy, light, dense, floaty, hot, cold?

What thoughts are you thinking that are creating that feeling for you?

Narrow it down to a specific sentence:

Is that sentence factual (or an opinion)?
Is it true? Is it helpful to continue thinking it?

How would you like to feel?

What thought could you think to feel that way?

Reflections:

date:

What specific feeling are you feeling right now?

Describe it. Where is it in your body?
Is it fast, slow, heavy, light, dense, floaty, hot, cold?

What thoughts are you thinking that are creating that feeling for you?

Narrow it down to a specific sentence:

Is that sentence factual (or an opinion)?
Is it true? Is it helpful to continue thinking it?

How would you like to feel?

What thought could you think to feel that way?

Reflections:

date:

What specific feeling are you feeling right now?

Describe it. Where is it in your body?
Is it fast, slow, heavy, light, dense, floaty, hot, cold?

What thoughts are you thinking that are creating that feeling for you?

Narrow it down to a specific sentence:

Is that sentence factual (or an opinion)?
Is it true? Is it helpful to continue thinking it?

How would you like to feel?

What thought could you think to feel that way?

Reflections:

date:

What specific feeling are you feeling right now?

Describe it. Where is it in your body?
Is it fast, slow, heavy, light, dense, floaty, hot, cold?

What thoughts are you thinking that are creating that feeling for you?

Narrow it down to a specific sentence:

Is that sentence factual (or an opinion)?
Is it true? Is it helpful to continue thinking it?

How would you like to feel?

What thought could you think to feel that way?

Reflections:

date:

What specific feeling are you feeling right now?

Describe it. Where is it in your body?
Is it fast, slow, heavy, light, dense, floaty, hot, cold?

What thoughts are you thinking that are creating that feeling for you?

Narrow it down to a specific sentence:

Is that sentence factual (or an opinion)?
Is it true? Is it helpful to continue thinking it?

How would you like to feel?

What thought could you think to feel that way?

Reflections:

date:

What specific feeling are you feeling right now?

Describe it. Where is it in your body?
Is it fast, slow, heavy, light, dense, floaty, hot, cold?

What thoughts are you thinking that are creating that feeling for you?

Narrow it down to a specific sentence:

Is that sentence factual (or an opinion)?
Is it true? Is it helpful to continue thinking it?

How would you like to feel?

What thought could you think to feel that way?

Reflections:

date:

What specific feeling are you feeling right now?

Describe it. Where is it in your body?
Is it fast, slow, heavy, light, dense, floaty, hot, cold?

What thoughts are you thinking that are creating that feeling for you?

Narrow it down to a specific sentence:

Is that sentence factual (or an opinion)?
Is it true? Is it helpful to continue thinking it?

How would you like to feel?

What thought could you think to feel that way?

Reflections:

date:

What specific feeling are you feeling right now?

Describe it. Where is it in your body?
Is it fast, slow, heavy, light, dense, floaty, hot, cold?

What thoughts are you thinking that are creating that feeling for you?

Narrow it down to a specific sentence:

Is that sentence factual (or an opinion)?
Is it true? Is it helpful to continue thinking it?

How would you like to feel?

What thought could you think to feel that way?

Reflections:

date:

What specific feeling are you feeling right now?

Describe it. Where is it in your body?
Is it fast, slow, heavy, light, dense, floaty, hot, cold?

What thoughts are you thinking that are creating that feeling for you?

Narrow it down to a specific sentence:

Is that sentence factual (or an opinion)?
Is it true? Is it helpful to continue thinking it?

How would you like to feel?

What thought could you think to feel that way?

Reflections:

date:

What specific feeling are you feeling right now?

Describe it. Where is it in your body?
Is it fast, slow, heavy, light, dense, floaty, hot, cold?

What thoughts are you thinking that are creating that feeling for you?

Narrow it down to a specific sentence:

Is that sentence factual (or an opinion)?
Is it true? Is it helpful to continue thinking it?

How would you like to feel?

What thought could you think to feel that way?

Reflections:

date:

What specific feeling are you feeling right now?

Describe it. Where is it in your body?
Is it fast, slow, heavy, light, dense, floaty, hot, cold?

What thoughts are you thinking that are creating that feeling for you?

Narrow it down to a specific sentence:

Is that sentence factual (or an opinion)?
Is it true? Is it helpful to continue thinking it?

How would you like to feel?

What thought could you think to feel that way?

Reflections:

date:

What specific feeling are you feeling right now?

Describe it. Where is it in your body?
Is it fast, slow, heavy, light, dense, floaty, hot, cold?

What thoughts are you thinking that are creating that feeling for you?

Narrow it down to a specific sentence:

Is that sentence factual (or an opinion)?
Is it true? Is it helpful to continue thinking it?

How would you like to feel?

What thought could you think to feel that way?

Reflections:

date:

What specific feeling are you feeling right now?

Describe it. Where is it in your body?
Is it fast, slow, heavy, light, dense, floaty, hot, cold?

What thoughts are you thinking that are creating that feeling for you?

Narrow it down to a specific sentence:

Is that sentence factual (or an opinion)?
Is it true? Is it helpful to continue thinking it?

How would you like to feel?

What thought could you think to feel that way?

Reflections:

date:

What specific feeling are you feeling right now?

Describe it. Where is it in your body?
Is it fast, slow, heavy, light, dense, floaty, hot, cold?

What thoughts are you thinking that are creating that feeling for you?

Narrow it down to a specific sentence:

Is that sentence factual (or an opinion)?
Is it true? Is it helpful to continue thinking it?

How would you like to feel?

What thought could you think to feel that way?

Reflections:

date:

What specific feeling are you feeling right now?

Describe it. Where is it in your body?
Is it fast, slow, heavy, light, dense, floaty, hot, cold?

What thoughts are you thinking that are creating that feeling for you?

Narrow it down to a specific sentence:

Is that sentence factual (or an opinion)?
Is it true? Is it helpful to continue thinking it?

How would you like to feel?

What thought could you think to feel that way?

Reflections:

date:

What specific feeling are you feeling right now?

Describe it. Where is it in your body?
Is it fast, slow, heavy, light, dense, floaty, hot, cold?

What thoughts are you thinking that are creating that feeling for you?

Narrow it down to a specific sentence:

Is that sentence factual (or an opinion)?
Is it true? Is it helpful to continue thinking it?

How would you like to feel?

What thought could you think to feel that way?

Reflections:

date:

What specific feeling are you feeling right now?

Describe it. Where is it in your body?
Is it fast, slow, heavy, light, dense, floaty, hot, cold?

What thoughts are you thinking that are creating that feeling for you?

Narrow it down to a specific sentence:

Is that sentence factual (or an opinion)?
Is it true? Is it helpful to continue thinking it?

How would you like to feel?

What thought could you think to feel that way?

Reflections:

date:

What specific feeling are you feeling right now?

Describe it. Where is it in your body?
Is it fast, slow, heavy, light, dense, floaty, hot, cold?

What thoughts are you thinking that are creating that feeling for you?

Narrow it down to a specific sentence:

Is that sentence factual (or an opinion)?
Is it true? Is it helpful to continue thinking it?

How would you like to feel?

What thought could you think to feel that way?

Reflections:

date:

What specific feeling are you feeling right now?

Describe it. Where is it in your body?
Is it fast, slow, heavy, light, dense, floaty, hot, cold?

What thoughts are you thinking that are creating that feeling for you?

Narrow it down to a specific sentence:

Is that sentence factual (or an opinion)?
Is it true? Is it helpful to continue thinking it?

How would you like to feel?

What thought could you think to feel that way?

Reflections:

date:

What specific feeling are you feeling right now?

Describe it. Where is it in your body?
Is it fast, slow, heavy, light, dense, floaty, hot, cold?

What thoughts are you thinking that are creating that feeling for you?

Narrow it down to a specific sentence:

Is that sentence factual (or an opinion)?
Is it true? Is it helpful to continue thinking it?

How would you like to feel?

What thought could you think to feel that way?

Reflections:

date:

What specific feeling are you feeling right now?

Describe it. Where is it in your body?
Is it fast, slow, heavy, light, dense, floaty, hot, cold?

What thoughts are you thinking that are creating that feeling for you?

Narrow it down to a specific sentence:

Is that sentence factual (or an opinion)?
Is it true? Is it helpful to continue thinking it?

How would you like to feel?

What thought could you think to feel that way?

Reflections:

date:

What specific feeling are you feeling right now?

Describe it. Where is it in your body?
Is it fast, slow, heavy, light, dense, floaty, hot, cold?

What thoughts are you thinking that are creating that feeling for you?

Narrow it down to a specific sentence:

Is that sentence factual (or an opinion)?
Is it true? Is it helpful to continue thinking it?

How would you like to feel?

What thought could you think to feel that way?

Reflections:

date:

What specific feeling are you feeling right now?

Describe it. Where is it in your body?
Is it fast, slow, heavy, light, dense, floaty, hot, cold?

What thoughts are you thinking that are creating that feeling for you?

Narrow it down to a specific sentence:

Is that sentence factual (or an opinion)?
Is it true? Is it helpful to continue thinking it?

How would you like to feel?

What thought could you think to feel that way?

Reflections:

date:

What specific feeling are you feeling right now?

Describe it. Where is it in your body?
Is it fast, slow, heavy, light, dense, floaty, hot, cold?

What thoughts are you thinking that are creating that feeling for you?

Narrow it down to a specific sentence:

Is that sentence factual (or an opinion)?
Is it true? Is it helpful to continue thinking it?

How would you like to feel?

What thought could you think to feel that way?

Reflections:

date:

What specific feeling are you feeling right now?

Describe it. Where is it in your body?
Is it fast, slow, heavy, light, dense, floaty, hot, cold?

What thoughts are you thinking that are creating that feeling for you?

Narrow it down to a specific sentence:

Is that sentence factual (or an opinion)?
Is it true? Is it helpful to continue thinking it?

How would you like to feel?

What thought could you think to feel that way?

Reflections:

date:

What specific feeling are you feeling right now?

Describe it. Where is it in your body?
Is it fast, slow, heavy, light, dense, floaty, hot, cold?

What thoughts are you thinking that are creating that feeling for you?

Narrow it down to a specific sentence:

Is that sentence factual (or an opinion)?
Is it true? Is it helpful to continue thinking it?

How would you like to feel?

What thought could you think to feel that way?

Reflections:

date:

What specific feeling are you feeling right now?

Describe it. Where is it in your body?
Is it fast, slow, heavy, light, dense, floaty, hot, cold?

What thoughts are you thinking that are creating that feeling for you?

Narrow it down to a specific sentence:

Is that sentence factual (or an opinion)?
Is it true? Is it helpful to continue thinking it?

How would you like to feel?

What thought could you think to feel that way?

Reflections:

date:

What specific feeling are you feeling right now?

Describe it. Where is it in your body?
Is it fast, slow, heavy, light, dense, floaty, hot, cold?

What thoughts are you thinking that are creating that feeling for you?

Narrow it down to a specific sentence:

Is that sentence factual (or an opinion)?
Is it true? Is it helpful to continue thinking it?

How would you like to feel?

What thought could you think to feel that way?

Reflections:

date:

What specific feeling are you feeling right now?

Describe it. Where is it in your body?
Is it fast, slow, heavy, light, dense, floaty, hot, cold?

What thoughts are you thinking that are creating that feeling for you?

Narrow it down to a specific sentence:

Is that sentence factual (or an opinion)?
Is it true? Is it helpful to continue thinking it?

How would you like to feel?

What thought could you think to feel that way?

Reflections:

date:

What specific feeling are you feeling right now?

Describe it. Where is it in your body?
Is it fast, slow, heavy, light, dense, floaty, hot, cold?

What thoughts are you thinking that are creating that feeling for you?

Narrow it down to a specific sentence:

Is that sentence factual (or an opinion)?
Is it true? Is it helpful to continue thinking it?

How would you like to feel?

What thought could you think to feel that way?

Reflections:

date:

What specific feeling are you feeling right now?

Describe it. Where is it in your body?
Is it fast, slow, heavy, light, dense, floaty, hot, cold?

What thoughts are you thinking that are creating that feeling for you?

Narrow it down to a specific sentence:

Is that sentence factual (or an opinion)?
Is it true? Is it helpful to continue thinking it?

How would you like to feel?

What thought could you think to feel that way?

Reflections:

date:

What specific feeling are you feeling right now?

Describe it. Where is it in your body?
Is it fast, slow, heavy, light, dense, floaty, hot, cold?

What thoughts are you thinking that are creating that feeling for you?

Narrow it down to a specific sentence:

Is that sentence factual (or an opinion)?
Is it true? Is it helpful to continue thinking it?

How would you like to feel?

What thought could you think to feel that way?

Reflections:

date:

What specific feeling are you feeling right now?

Describe it. Where is it in your body?
Is it fast, slow, heavy, light, dense, floaty, hot, cold?

What thoughts are you thinking that are creating that feeling for you?

Narrow it down to a specific sentence:

Is that sentence factual (or an opinion)?
Is it true? Is it helpful to continue thinking it?

How would you like to feel?

What thought could you think to feel that way?

Reflections:

date:

What specific feeling are you feeling right now?

Describe it. Where is it in your body?
Is it fast, slow, heavy, light, dense, floaty, hot, cold?

What thoughts are you thinking that are creating that feeling for you?

Narrow it down to a specific sentence:

Is that sentence factual (or an opinion)?
Is it true? Is it helpful to continue thinking it?

How would you like to feel?

What thought could you think to feel that way?

Reflections:

date:

What specific feeling are you feeling right now?

Describe it. Where is it in your body?
Is it fast, slow, heavy, light, dense, floaty, hot, cold?

What thoughts are you thinking that are creating that feeling for you?

Narrow it down to a specific sentence:

Is that sentence factual (or an opinion)?
Is it true? Is it helpful to continue thinking it?

How would you like to feel?

What thought could you think to feel that way?

Reflections:

date:

What specific feeling are you feeling right now?

Describe it. Where is it in your body?
Is it fast, slow, heavy, light, dense, floaty, hot, cold?

What thoughts are you thinking that are creating that feeling for you?

Narrow it down to a specific sentence:

Is that sentence factual (or an opinion)?
Is it true? Is it helpful to continue thinking it?

How would you like to feel?

What thought could you think to feel that way?

Reflections:

date:

What specific feeling are you feeling right now?

Describe it. Where is it in your body?
Is it fast, slow, heavy, light, dense, floaty, hot, cold?

What thoughts are you thinking that are creating that feeling for you?

Narrow it down to a specific sentence:

Is that sentence factual (or an opinion)?
Is it true? Is it helpful to continue thinking it?

How would you like to feel?

What thought could you think to feel that way?

Reflections:

date:

What specific feeling are you feeling right now?

Describe it. Where is it in your body?
Is it fast, slow, heavy, light, dense, floaty, hot, cold?

What thoughts are you thinking that are creating that feeling for you?

Narrow it down to a specific sentence:

Is that sentence factual (or an opinion)?
Is it true? Is it helpful to continue thinking it?

How would you like to feel?

What thought could you think to feel that way?

Reflections:

date:

What specific feeling are you feeling right now?

Describe it. Where is it in your body?
Is it fast, slow, heavy, light, dense, floaty, hot, cold?

What thoughts are you thinking that are creating that feeling for you?

Narrow it down to a specific sentence:

Is that sentence factual (or an opinion)?
Is it true? Is it helpful to continue thinking it?

How would you like to feel?

What thought could you think to feel that way?

Reflections:

date:

What specific feeling are you feeling right now?

Describe it. Where is it in your body?
Is it fast, slow, heavy, light, dense, floaty, hot, cold?

What thoughts are you thinking that are creating that feeling for you?

Narrow it down to a specific sentence:

Is that sentence factual (or an opinion)?
Is it true? Is it helpful to continue thinking it?

How would you like to feel?

What thought could you think to feel that way?

Reflections:

Hey There!
You made it to the end.

(or you flipped back here before you even started the book)

Congratulations on feeling all those feelings!

Are you ready for another notebook or journal? Grab another one of these and/or look for other journals, diaries and notebooks also available.

For example:

-A Daily 3-minute Gratitude Journal
to quickly notice things you're so appreciative of (and reflect on longer if you have more than 3 minutes)

-A Dream Interpretation Journal
to train your brain to remember your dreams and figure out their meanings

-A Bright Ideas and Brainstorms Notebook
to collect all your best insights

And so many more!
Just go to bexb.org/shopjournals to see them all.

Made in the USA
Las Vegas, NV
15 December 2023